Too Stuck to Move

How NOT to be a Vainglorious, Haughty, Arrogant, Patronizing, Immodest, Conceited, Egocentric, Condescending, Generationally Privileged, Passive-aggressive, Self-important, Self-opinionated, Self-Satisfied, Blameshifting Stick up Your Butt Narcissist — in the Workplace

Brien Norris

53
YEAR

ISBN 978-0-9818612-1-0 (paperback)

Library of Congress Control Number: 2018903475

Organizations wanting to purchase larger quantities for training purposes are encouraged to contact the author to inquire about volume discounts. Email BrienNorris1@gmail.com.

Published by 53 Year Publishing

Edited by Nancy Cole

Book Cover Design & Illustrations by Brien Norris

Table of Contents

Introduction

Are you a Vainglorious, Haughty, Arrogant, Patronizing, Immodest, Conceited, Egocentric, Condescending, Generationally Privileged, Passive-aggressive, Self-important, Self-opinionated, Self-Satisfied Blameshifting, Stick up Your Butt Narcissist?

Let's find out!

How does a person get to the point where some or all of these words accurately describe them?

It's like keeping clothes from years past in your closet that you'll never wear again. Even though these garments don't fit you or are too outdated to wear in public, you can't bring yourself to throw them out, donate them or re-purpose them.

In your head, you conclude that you spent too much money on these clothes. Or, you feel they have sentimental value. So, you hold on to them. You find new places to store them, plus devise new ways to sort and label them. You have organized clothing at least, right? But you won't get rid of your unneeded clothes. When it comes time to move, your collection of clothing becomes a costly liability.

Another analogy

Your house is full of items that are unused, packed in boxes or functionally obsolete but have memories attached to them. You got this tchotchke on a trip 20 years ago, when you were happier. You won this trophy or certificate for coming in second for Spirit Day. It's dusty or yellowed, but something about it reminds you of a teacher who encouraged you or perhaps, a friend who no longer calls you.

You'd be better off jettisoning all your stuff, but it's too hard to let go of the memories and too painful logistically to pick it all up and have someone haul it away.

Similarly, you have a garage or storage shed full of old tools that have seen better days. Broken blades and drill bits. Frayed cords. Burnt out bulbs and dead batteries. Unstarted or unfinished projects relegated to dusty dark corners. Manuals for stuff you no longer have. Tools that at some point served a useful function. Things you once used to fix, improve, and build.

Now imagine these places packed with shelves of your ideas about the world, about work and people. On the ledge to the left sits the box of pride. It contains all types of pride; the pride you take in winning promotions and being voted best so and so for three years running. It's also filled with pride in your nationality, your gender, your age (either the abundance of, or lack of it), your degrees, your real-world smarts, and your intellect.

Your box also contains the pride you derive from your belongings and status.

It's a massive box!

You've managed to pack it with the cumulative pride and self-assurance derived from your tastes in politics, music and technology providers.

That box carries the satisfaction you derive from your abilities; occupational, sports, parenting, pet-rearing, artistic, writing, gardening, drink-making, cooking, math, negotiation, thriftiness, seductive skills and powers of persuasion.

Your box of pride becomes immovable because it bulges with the pride you take from being better, more right, more enlightened, more selfless, more politically correct and more forgiving than other people.

Top your box off with the pride you take in your (more morally correct or less caloric) food choices, energy consumption choices or more rational use of technology than others.

Are you getting a sense of how massive that box can get? Now add more weight.

With the pride you take in your diverse abilities also comes the memories of how it feels to be right, to be the problem-solver, to be known as the consistent one, the one with their head screwed on straight, the mature one, the creative one, or the one with the answers.

No matter how much time passes, the memories of the past make you crave the golden years. You want another hit. So you try to keep things the way they were when you were able to bask in the glow of your reputation and abilities. You do things in the present to try to get the sense of satisfaction that your abilities gave you back in the day.

Perhaps you actively or passively prevent people from taking the spotlight. Or you create rules that force people to include you in every decision. You insist on mandates requiring your input, signature, a stamp of approval, creative spin or royal proclamation.

Sometimes your pride creates a yearning for relevance, respect, and reverence. This craving makes you do things like: talking about others behind their back, repeating unsubstantiated claims, or even making stuff up, all to make yourself look good in comparison.

Or you look for people to fix, heal, and save, to be seen as loving, kind and benevolent. You use the role of healer to cloak the feeling of emptiness you experience when you aren't being praised, glorified and used as an example of what it means to be a virtuous person. People question your motives and sense your insincerity, and you dare to wonder why.

And that's just one box!

In another box on the shelf in your storage shed, you'll find the "Not Me!" stick. The "Not Me!" stick formed from all the times you've refused to hold yourself accountable for your own mistakes.

The issue here isn't about being human and messing up. Mistakes and failure happen, and we learn from them; they make us stronger and wiser.

The thing that weighs you down **is the history of denial**. Every time you shun responsibility for messing up or shift the blame to someone else or something else – when you know that you were the one who perpetuated the failure – the "Not Me" stick lengthens, along with its gravity.

Perhaps your parents told you how perfect you were as a child. Unfortunately, you believed them and as a result, refuse to see that you can and will fumble on occasion. Or maybe you were punished so severely early in life for confessing your foibles, that you've decided that "coming clean" is not in your best interest. In place of a backbone, you need your stick to prop you up!

Your failure, refusal, or inability to own your mistakes has real-world ramifications. Reset buttons don't exist in the real world, but you can apologize and try to make it right. You can get training, develop systems or seek out skilled mentors to lower the likelihood of future failure. In your world, those are not even options, because nothing is ever your fault.

Your penchant for pointing fingers at external factors defines you, making you appear cowardly. You live under the delusion of invincibility, and it hurts everyone around you. This weighty box of sticks makes getting stuck likely. It complicates the task of finding people willing to work with you, be on a team with you or take direction from you.

Shine a flashlight in your storage shed. You're likely to find several boxes next to the Pride and "Not Me!" each with a unique name. The Narcissist Box. The "Stick up Your Butt" Box. The Conceit Box. And so on, until you realize the magnitude of your collection. One tote is heavy. It only takes a few totes to crush you.

Do you want your tombstone to read:

"Here lies a Vainglorious, Haughty, Arrogant, Patronizing, Immodest, Conceited, Egocentric, Condescending, Generationally Privileged, Passive-aggressive, Self-important, Self-opinionated, Self-Satisfied, Blameshifting, Stick up Your Butt Narcissist."?

It only takes one long, heavy stick to immobilize you. Even when presented with an alternative, some people become too stuck to move. Without self-evaluation, you aren't even aware of how unable to move you've become. Like a scarecrow on a stick in a cornfield, you get impaled by a stick held together by complacency.

It's a stick that gets longer as the years go on and you keep justifying the way you do things, how you treat others and how you perceive the world.

You get stuck because you start loving yourself too much and stop seeking out new ideas, alternate ways of doing things and different ways to express yourself.

When you get stuck, you end up loathing, even attacking, anyone or anything that challenges the cement of self-satisfaction poured around your feet. You become incapacitated by fear and outdated thinking. You freeze in place, held still by the fear that your poorly constructed legacy will unravel.

Meanwhile, the people you care about either move on or you get stuck in unhealthy relationships. The companies you work at either advance without you (because you are "let go," phased out, replaced, or quarantined to a dead-end position). Or your organizations fail, in part, because the people you work with are just as stuck as you are.

People say that you can't manage what you can't measure. If you can't shine a light on the "boxes" in your storage shed and see them for what they are, then how can you expect to move forward?

This book is designed to help you regain your freedom to move around and lighten the load. I'm always working on myself. I know what it feels like to be boxed in by your own inflated sense of self-worth and the pain of trying to prune back pride that should never have been allowed to grow so freely to begin with.

In the process, you'll learn how NOT be a Vainglorious, Haughty, Arrogant, Patronizing, Immodest, Conceited, Egocentric, Condescending, Generationally

Privileged, Passive-aggressive, Self-important, Self-opinionated, Self-Satisfied, Blameshifting, Stick up Your Butt Narcissist.

As a writer, corporate trainer and facilitator, I've been fortunate to speak at companies in every state in the United States and every province in Canada. That experience has given me a unique insight into the most common obstacles dealt with at work and home.

That's why I created the STICK Survey. I wanted to give audiences and readers (and myself) a measurable way to assess their beliefs and values and to identify patterns that cause adverse outcomes.

As extreme as some of the words listed above may seem, they are actually a nicer set of descriptors than what you may be more accustomed to being called.

Answer just 40 statements and scenarios, and you're on your way to changing the least flattering aspects of yourself. Whether your goal is surviving change, getting people to work together, or dealing with the negativity prevalent in the workplace, the reality is the same. **We can't change others. We can only change ourselves.**

I've had the opportunity to personally give The STICK Survey to thousands of men and women across North America. I've been able to tweak each item on the survey so that when it's complete, you'll have a good idea of your strengths and weaknesses.

The scenarios and statements have been vetted by people in virtually every industry and occupation at every level from front-line staff to executives. The results of this survey are tested and consistent. You'll find the STICK Survey extremely useful for personal development – and ultimately liberating.

Armed with your honest answers and new insights, you'll have a real opportunity to get unstuck. Use the contents of this book to capture an at-the-moment snapshot of who you are, what you believe, and how those beliefs affect you and your coworkers. Use the ideas found in these pages to engage in the shift in thinking required to free yourself from those boxes and sticks.

You don't have to be the scarecrow. That stick need not be your death sentence.

The STICK Survey

How to Answer

For each of the following 40 statements, scenarios or questions, please answer by writing a :

2 for yes

1 for sometimes

0 for no.

in the space below each statement or scenario. (or on a separate piece of paper if you are viewing this as an e-book.)

IMPORTANT!

Answer each statement or scenario according to the way YOU genuinely feel or do most of the time in a **work setting**.

Resist the urge to answer based on what the politically correct response might be, or what you guess the social expectation might be.

Consider each statement, scenario or question and think about how you feel at a gut level.

12

QUESTIONS AND SCENARIOS

2 = yes   1 = sometimes   0 = no

1. You know that you've learned everything you need to know about doing your job and succeeding in life.

_____

2. When you disagree with what someone says you tend to roll your eyes, shrug, or smirk (either to their face or when they're not looking at you).

_____

3. You mimic or exaggerate the words or facial expressions of people you disagree with or don't like (either to their face or when gossiping with others).

_____

4. When in a conversation with others, you feel you have to modify your vocabulary and tone of voice to make them understand what you have to say.

_____

5. (You believe that) managers are supposed to intuitively know what's wrong or what "needs fixing" to begin with because that's what they get paid to do. That's why you refrain from telling management about problems you've observed or specific feedback or suggestions you've received from customers.

_____

6. Specific rules like attendance and accountability shouldn't apply to you, just other people at work and home.

_____

7. If only there were more people like you, the world would be a better place.

_____

8. You quote from your company's policy manual and let others know when they are not following procedure or not doing something exactly right.

_____

9. Not showing up early or staying after 5 pm to finish work demonstrates a lack of dedication to the organization.

_____

10. Your way is the only right way to do anything.

_____

2 = yes   1 = sometimes   0 = no

11. If you want something done right, you have to do it yourself.

_____

12. We should follow traditions religiously. We've always done it this way, and that's how we're going to keep doing it. So, don't ask why!

_____

13. (You feel that) everyone is jealous of you. People always do things to make your life more difficult.

_____

14. If it weren't for a particular person or group of people, you'd be more successful and able to accomplish all the things you've ever dreamed of doing.

_____

15. The best way to show people how you feel is to sabotage a project by stalling, refusing to participate or withholding information.

_____

16. If it's not your idea, then it's not worth looking at or implementing.

_____

17. You tend to interrupt questions or stop people in the middle of their comments.

_____

18. If it's not in your written job description, then it's not your responsibility.

_____

19. People should know what we expect of them, and what we're thinking. After all, it's their job!

_____

20. You have a right to yell, insult and berate others, or physically assault them if they upset you or you don't get your way.

_____

2 = yes   1 = sometimes   0 = no

21. You can't trust people to work (or do what you've asked them to do) without constant supervision.

_____

22. The best results come through micro-managing the actions of every person involved with a task, project or assignment.

_____

23. The process is more important than the outcome.

_____

24. People should respect you because you've paid your dues.

_____

25. People should immediately respect you because of your life experiences.

_____

26. People should respect you because you're the boss and you've got the title to prove it.

_____

27. If it ain't broke, don't fix it.

_____

28. Other people always have stupid ideas that would never work and aren't worth your attention.

_____

29. Spontaneity is foolish.

_____

30. Before presenting an idea, you must plan every word you're going to say and stick to it, no matter what.

_____

2 = yes   1 = sometimes   0 = no

31. If a task has not been entered into your daily calendar or on your to-do list, then you won't do it.

_____

32. Asking for assistance from others is a sign of weakness.

_____

33. If someone doesn't agree with you, then that person has a severe mental problem.

_____

34. Your winning personality is all you need to get by in any situation.

_____

35. It's all about facts. People should agree with you because you know more than they do. You've got the degree, certification, and experience to prove it.

_____

36. There's a place for everything, and everything should be in its place.

_____

37. We should avoid change because things are fine just the way they are.

_____

38. Why can't things be like the good old days?

_____

39. It's not your job to ask questions. If people have a problem, they'll let you know about it.

_____

40. If people dedicate themselves to their jobs, then they don't need on-going incentives or motivation.

_____

ONCE YOU'VE COMPLETED THE STICK SURVEY

1. Add up your scores.

Enter your total score here (or on the piece of paper you've been using to keep scores)

_____

2. Divide your overall count by 2 and round up to the next whole number.

Enter your new score here (or on the piece of paper you've been using to keep scores).

_____

This final score indicates the length of your "stick" and provides a starting point for reflection and improvement.

Continue to the following pages to see what the results mean.

RESULTS

Read on to discover what your score means.

A SCORE OF 10 OR HIGHER

DANGER!

Long sticks can lead to long-term problems. It's a good time to re-evaluate your belief systems, perspectives, and ego. These and other issues may be holding you back, fostering a negative workplace, creating anxiety and angst or altogether repelling people away from you.

Review the statements again and identify areas where your current views may be hindering your growth, success, and performance.

Take some time now to read and work through the Review section that follows. If getting unstuck on your own seems impossible, be brave enough to seek out mentors or work with a coach or therapist for extra support.

A SCORE OF 9

BORDERLINE!!

People with long sticks get left behind as the world, relationships and opportunities seek more adaptable people. What are your sticking points? Read through the next section and look for ways to manage yourself so that you stay flexible and positive.

A SCORE OF 6 TO 8

AVERAGE.

North American scores average between 6 to 8. Don't be satisfied with getting an average score. Resist complacency. You can do better! We measure improvement in inches, not feet or miles. Revisit the statements in the following section and create an action plan based on what you can do right now to manage your thoughts, actions, and interaction skills proactively.

A SCORE OF 4 TO 5

WELL DONE!

A score of 4 to 5 is optimal. Congratulations. Your current score indicates you have achieved a balance in your life and how you live it. You can live in the present. You can manage or altogether eliminate your ego or need to be right.

You possess the fluidity to change and the focus to do what's necessary within a given framework. You understand the need to communicate and take action, rather than assume and do nothing.

You have an excellent attitude. You've evolved enough to know that it's acceptable to admit when you don't know everything and ask for help when appropriate. Finally, your score highlights your ability to trust and to be trusted.

Focus on being consistent, taking calculated risks and modeling appropriate behaviors for others.

A SCORE OF 3 OR UNDER

SKEPTIC ALERT!

You're either a saint or a liar (you choose!). While a low score might indicate that you've learned some valuable lessons early in life, it might also suggest that you picked "No" because you thought it was the best answer.

I designed The STICK Survey to garner at least a few "sometimes" from the balanced person. A zero response may indicate that a general apathy (I don't care) has crept into your life. It's one thing to be adaptable, easy going and open to change. It's another thing not to care or not to take a stand on anything.

REVISIT & REVIEW

1. You know that you've learned everything you need to know about doing your job and succeeding in life.

Everything? With the stunning rate of change taking place every day, combined with the incredible wealth of new information discovered and disseminated each day, it's virtually impossible that any of us know everything we need to know about doing our jobs and succeeding in life.

You might be an expert on your subject because of your education. You might be an expert by having lots of life experience. The real expert is the one who commits to being a life-long learner. Whether it's through reading, listening, observing or practicing, the life-long learner finds a way to improve themselves daily.

No matter what skills got you to where you are, there are still undiscovered ways or untapped methodologies to tweak what you do and how you do it, especially in the game of life.

Questions:

What have you done in the past week to improve yourself at work?

How have you used your knowledge and skills to help someone else?

2. When you disagree with what someone says, you tend to roll your eyes, shrug, or smirk (either to their face or when they're not looking at you).

Anger, frustration, and impatience are natural parts of the human experience. It's also highly likely that you're going to disagree with what someone says, and that someone is going to disagree with you. So it's understandable to respond to this statement with a "sometimes." Eye rolling and smirking are far better than strangling or mortally wounding someone.

Still, a tell-tale sign of maturity is how we communicate with others. Just because you disagree doesn't mean you should disregard their opinions altogether or use non-verbal responses to shut down or discredit the person speaking. Disrespect need not be the default response when interacting with others.

There are better ways than using juvenile body language to disagree with someone whose ideas don't align with yours. When the eye rolling, shrugging and smirking become automatic responses, it's an indicator that you're having some self-esteem issues or have some gaps in your belief systems.

Furthermore, not everyone you meet is a conceited, pompous jerk. Not everyone is out to hurt you or embarrass you. Many of the people you interact with legitimately want to help you and teach you to improve.

The way they go about doing it may cause your defenses to go up and your ability to take in new information go down. Especially, if what they're saying is patently false or delivered in a judgmental, defensive or condescending tone.

Instead of the passive aggressive behavior, speak up and let the person you're talking to know how you prefer to be instructed or given feedback.

A person who can listen is highly desirable. So is a person who can control their emotions. Learn to manage your inner critic.

When you can take feedback from someone (regardless of their age or status) without getting defensive, you open yourself to the possibility of streamlining the learning process by being able to live and learn through someone else's error.

Questions:

What assumptions might be preventing you from engaging with people who hold differing positions or perspectives?

Are you a prisoner to your emotions? If so, what can you do to strengthen your self-control?

3. You mimic or exaggerate the words or facial expressions of people you disagree with or don't like (either to their face or when gossiping with others).

There are two issues to consider with this statement.

First, immaturity is an unwelcome quality. The immature person resorts to insults, mockery and name-calling because they cannot respond with integrity. The naive person also fails to understand the litigious ramifications that such behavior can cause for themselves and for the company that issues their paycheck.

Conversely, the mature person learns how to communicate honestly **without** having to resort to sophomoric behavior like making fun of the person you dislike or disagree with.

Secondly, few things will stall your career faster than being known as a gossiper. If you can't say it to their face, you shouldn't say it at all. If you've heard a rumor through the grapevine, let what you've listened to die on the vine.

Additionally, gossip is not the way to retaliate against someone with whom you disagree. If you meet privately and vocalize your point of view to the person or people you have a beef with, keep the outcome of those conversations private (unless the law requires transparency). Demonstrate the quality of your character by keeping the details of your quarrels secret.

Keep unsubstantiated rumors to yourself. If you really must know whether something is real, go to the source. Ask privately and non-judgmentally. Be prepared to get an "it's none of your business" as a response. If the source confides in you, honor their trust by shutting up, even when goaded by fellow gossipers.

Consider the political capital you'll have to spend once word gets around (and it always does) that you've been talking about or ridiculing someone behind their back. Is it worth it? How can you expect people to trust you or to see you as a person of integrity?

Questions:

When was the last time you were able to keep a secret?

Have you ever had someone make fun of you or quote you out of context?

How did you feel?

What are three things you can do to encourage a public dialogue in an environment where people feel safe in being able to voice their discontent or disagreement?

Have you ever put a mirror on your desk so that you can observe your body language during a conversation with someone else?

4. While conversing with others, you feel you have to modify your vocabulary and tone of voice to make them understand what you have to say.

Unless there is a legitimate language or educational gap between you and the people you are communicating with, refrain from treating someone like a child.

Even children should be spoken to in a normal voice using everyday words. Show everyone courtesy. Never assume that you'll have to change how you interact with another based on the negative experience you had with someone else in the past.

If you have a history of problems or conflict with the person you're speaking with, change the medium you use. Use email instead of the phone. Use visuals instead of words. Switch to face-to-face interactions instead of sending them memos.

Each of us has a different preferred way of receiving and sharing information. Have you asked the people around how they prefer to receive and process instructions? Have you told people how you like to get information?

If lots of people look at you with a bewildered look, you may be guilty of speaking too fast, not enunciating or using conflicting body language. Even worse, you may be guilty of using vocabulary words beyond the comprehension of your audience.

While your mastery of high-level words is admirable, no one walks around with a thesaurus. Using a 5th to 8th-grade speaking and writing level are optimal in most workplaces. What's the simplest, clearest way you can communicate your message?

It's not what you say, but how you say it.

5. A manager is supposed to intuitively know what's wrong or what "needs fixing" to begin with because that's what they get paid to do. That's why you refrain from telling management about problems you've observed or specific feedback or suggestions from customers.

Managers are not omnipresent or omnipotent. Additionally, management gets paid to get results through you. They are there to coach, mentor, and counsel you. They are there to make sure that the systems are in place that help create consistency and a safe working environment.

Don't let envy, fear or outdated ideas about what management already knows keep you from sharing information with your supervisors. If you want the perceived "status" sometimes associated with holding a management position, then you have to be willing to take on the responsibility of getting specific results. Do you want that responsibility?

Besides, improving a faulty process or a system is in everyone's best interest. Your position affords you a perspective, an opportunity, and responsibility.

Instead of being removed from the relentless machinery of business, you are fortunate to exist between the moving parts responsible for making work happen. You see what works and what doesn't. You get to see what's not getting done, but also get to revel in the daily successes. You get to deal firsthand with the maddening bureaucracy that lousy systems create.

The layer between you and customers is so minimal that you get to hear things firsthand, unfiltered and unrehearsed. With that proximity comes a fantastic opportunity to be a catalyst for positive change. You get to be an earpiece for the organization.

Are all managers great? No. Some have no business being in a management role. Do all managers seek out your feedback and ideas? No. But as long as you've made an effort to communicate a problem or pass on feedback from others in a professional way, you're holding up your end of the bargain.

Questions

Is there something that customers keep complaining about that seems to have escaped the notice of management?

Are you noticing a weak link in the process of how something gets ordered, in the way information gets shared with vendors or accounting, or in the treatment of customers?

Are there issues affecting employee morale that might be addressed with some minor adjustments to the current way of doing things?

Who can you talk to?

When will you bring it up?

6. Specific rules like attendance and accountability shouldn't apply to you, just other people at work and home.

A rule is a shared expectation. If that rule is good for one person, then it should be good for everyone in that environment. Rules create order and consistency. If the expectation, for instance, is to show up on time, then show up on time. If the expectation is that people will be accountable for their decisions, regardless of how they turn out, then be accountable.

If a rule is unnecessary, then eliminate it. Otherwise – assuming that everyone knows the rules and have been trained to follow them – everyone should be expected to comply.

Questions

Are you guilty of using rules arbitrarily against people you dislike or to punish people who don't revere you?

If so, what does that behavior say about you?

Are there rules that can be purged from the policy manual or erased permanently from your organization's Standard Operating Procedures?

What can you do to hold yourself accountable and put the concept of fairness for all into place?

Are there rules that disappear once a person meets a certain performance criteria? Does everyone know about these exceptions and thresholds?

7. If only there were more people like you, the world would be a better place.

This one could **almost** warrant a sometimes. As pleasant as you are, the world doesn't need more than one of anybody. More people like you would diminish your individuality and detract from all the things that make you unique.

You can share your passions and ideologies with others. If you have a particular philosophy or worldview, then your actions should be enough to motivate others to believe as you do. The complexity of personalities that fill the world adds to the diversity of life.

Questions:

How specifically would the world be a better place if there were more people just like you?

What attributes about yourself make you exceptional?

What are five things you wish others would do more to follow the example you set?

What are five things **other** people do that you could benefit from if you emulate them?

How does a diverse workplace make things better, easier and more interesting?

8. You quote from your company's policy manual and let others know when they are not following procedure or not doing something exactly right.

There are right and wrong ways to correct people or to remind people that they are not following procedures.

Quoting from a book or policy manual rarely provokes the desired response. In fact, the worst way to teach a person the importance of following a multi-page policy to the letter is to rub non-compliance in their face.

You don't win a prize for committing policies and procedures to memory. Especially, when you memorize so that you can play "Gotcha!" all day long.

Doing a job well is in everyone's interest. When a co-worker falls short, it can be a teaching moment when handled tactfully. That's why we always should criticize in private. Unless you're willing to work with people who resent you and actively support your termination, exercise some sensitivity when providing feedback.

Before sounding the alarm when you observe someone filling out a form incorrectly, or taking too long to respond to your inquiry, or not using a software program or piece of equipment optimally, **ask yourself the following**:

In the big picture, who did their failure to comply hurt?

Did it create a harmful or dismal customer, client, patient, or donor experience?

Was there a real economic or cataclysmic consequence?

Was the lack of thoroughness or response time deliberate?

Was the oversight or missing check mark caused by any number of real-world issues that exist in the workplace, ones that a policy, form or procedure can't take into account?

Finally look at your private motivations.

What fuels your fervent drive to create, police and prop up bureaucracy? How far will you go to make sure things get done by the book, all the time?

Is your self-appointed role as Policy Evangelist just a ruse to exact revenge on people who out-rank or out-earn you? Is this your way to make up for the lack of fairness in your world?

43

Are you consistent regarding when, where, what, who and how you handle non-compliance? Or do you look away when friends or people with the same job title, within the same department or in the same union, church, or social circles commit similar policy gaffes?

Are you concerned with the success of your organization? Or are your "stick up your butt" proclivities a defense mechanism to push back against the general lack of control you have in your life? Or the anger and resentment you feel having to take direction from other people?

Are you better at policy-making than you are at interacting with human beings and forming real relationships?

What can you do differently to help a person do their job correctly or adhere to a policy more closely without creating resentment and harboring animosity?

If your intentions are pure, how can you demonstrate to people around you that you're trying to make the workplace safer, better, and stronger?

9. Not showing up early or staying after 5 pm to finish work demonstrates a lack of dedication to the organization.

People who arrive early and stay late aren't representative of model behavior. Instead, their practices are brilliant examples of poor time management and misplaced priorities. Workaholism is counterproductive and not something to be encouraged.

Organizations (and the managers within those groups) expecting employees to work beyond regular hours are guilty of antiquated thinking that positions human capital on the same level as office supplies – disposable resources.

Even worse, they're foolish to expect meaningful increases in productivity because of the Law of Diminishing Returns. The dedicated employee is the one who comes to work on time and puts in the effort required to accomplish all that is realistically possible within the span of time they put in. The dedicated employee self-monitors their health and refuses to put themselves into dangerous situations caused by overwork, lack of sleep, and lousy nutrition.

While deadlines may occasionally mandate staying after the traditional quitting time, the person who arrives on time and leaves on time demonstrates a saner approach to life balance.

Questions:

Are you setting unrealistic deadlines and completion dates?

What are you doing to ensure that the employee's eight-hours are as productive as possible?

When was the last time you and your staff or colleagues attended a time management or team building training program?

What incentives and consequences are in place to facilitate on-time completion and deter workaholism?

10. Your way is the only right way to do anything.

It may seem this way on many occasions. Sometimes, your approach really is the only right way to get things done correctly. In the workplace, your position may even mandate that people follow your way to the letter.

Still, is it possible that you're overgeneralizing? Is it possible that perhaps your way is just one of many ways to do "it"? The time it takes to do it might be longer than your way. It may even cost more or take more than one revision to accomplish what your approach may have achieved the first time. Few people learn through success. It is our failures, and the lessons we learn from them, that makes us stronger. Sometimes, it might be best to let them find out (and potentially fail) firsthand, especially, if no one solicited your opinion.

In your relationships, both at work and home, letting a person save face (not correcting them publicly, not harassing them for being less than perfect, giving them an opportunity to recognize their missteps and adjust on their own) is a desirable skill to have.

Try this.

Next time you're about to correct someone for not doing the task your way, wait seven seconds and think about how urgent it is for the person to ascribe to your approach.

48

11. If you want something done right, you have to do it yourself.

Another tough one! At first blush, it feels like the world is full of seemingly incompetent people who can't be trusted to do what they say they'll do. The reality is that for every person who lets you down, there are dozens of people who can be trusted to honor their commitments.

Additionally, before you can expect something to be done right, a few things have to happen.

First, the person you give a task or responsibility to has to be able to do what you've asked them to do.

Second, you have to be sure that your request is thoroughly understood. Are you communicating so that the person knows what you're asking?

Third, you have to trust them. Once you;

a) give the person or group specific instructions

b) have clarified your instructions and are confident they understand you

c) have confirmed that they have the knowledge, training and actual practice in doing what you've asked them to do,

You then have to the unthinkable. **You must step back!**

Reassure the person or group that you trust them and are confident in their ability to follow through. Expect people you work with to succeed. Spell out the parameters of your request.

When is it due?

What resources do they have to complete the request?

Who else do they have access to?

What are the legal or ethical constraints of your request?

Then, step back. Provide a supportive, but non-invasive role in allowing the person or team to succeed.

12. We should follow traditions religiously. We've always done it this way, and that's how we're going to keep doing it. So, don't ask why!

Certain traditions give us meaning, purpose and a solid epicenter around which we make our decisions. That said, not everyone is going to view your traditions or beliefs with the same reverence.

To a growing number of people, sacred cows make the best burgers! If you believe in something, you should be able to defend it without resorting to the "we've always done it this way" argument.

Asking "Why?" is a legitimate question too. You may agree to disagree if you choose. But our strengths as human beings lie in our ability to fuse our emotional and rational stance to make an informed decision.

Questions:

Why do I believe what I believe?

Are they my beliefs or someone else's?

What if we tried something different? Who would be hurt? Who might benefit?

Is there a possibility that there's room for multiple perspectives?

13. (You feel that) everyone is jealous of you. People always do things to make your life more difficult.

Be wary of the "everyone, always, no one, never" rationales. Human beings are infamous for our capacity to harbor jealousy, resentment, or hatred towards other people. We're even more renowned for our tendency to point fingers at others as a way of escaping personal accountability.

People who believe the "everyone is jealous of them" excuse have some severe challenges taking personal responsibility for their situation. You are the totality of your choices. The choices you've made in every area of your life are why you are where you are at this moment, and why you will be where you are in one week or one year from now.

You choose to speak up or to stay quiet. You decide to act or to do nothing. You want to work at something or to let it fall apart. You choose to rise above another person's spite or jealousy or to become a slave to it.

14. If it weren't for a particular person or group of people, you'd be more successful and able to accomplish all the things you've ever dreamed of doing.

Be sure to read the comments to statement #13, because they apply here too. The challenge with this one is that entire groups exist to reinforce the belief that certain people or organizations of people stand in the way of their success, or stifle their dreams.

We blame parents, lovers, children, and neighbors. We blame presidents, politics, religions, corporations, and lobbyists. We point the finger at entire groups of people of various ethnicities, melanin levels, accents and sexual orientations. Instead of finger pointing, it might be better (and more accurate) to ask a few questions:

Is my situation the by-product of laziness?

Why do I feel entitled to be given anything based solely on my age, race, religion, orientation, nationality, education, economic status or because of the pain my ancestors had to endure?

Who else has gone through what I'm going through and lived to talk about it?

How can I learn from their experiences?

What are my dreams?

What have I done today to make those dreams come true?

What would happen if I devoted half of the energy I spend blaming others for my situation to moving towards my goals, desires, and ambitions?

15. The best ways to show people how you feel are to sabotage a project by stalling, refusing to participate or withholding information.

We all probably know people who use these tactics. They may even seem to succeed in sending a clear message to the people left in the debris. What these tactics show people is that you're an immature, passive-aggressive brat with minimal backbone.

If someone or something bothers you – be it at work or home – the optimal thing to do is speak up, assert yourself and accept that you're not always going to get your way.

How do you assert yourself?

First, ask to speak with the person or group of people you have an issue with privately, if possible.

"Hey Bob, can we talk in private for a few minutes?"

Second, describe to them, using a measured tone and short sentences how you feel or what you think about whatever it is that's bothering you.

"I feel or think that this (decision, request or project) is a (bad one/unfair/lacks merit, etc.)."

Third, explain to the group in the same conversational tone, and with open, relaxed body language how their behaviors, actions or request affect you.

"When you ask me to get involved or to make a decision without giving me time to think about it or gather additional opinions you prevent me from doing a great job or make me feel like my opinions are not welcome."

Fourth, specify what you would like them to do, or the treatment or structure you prefer.

"I want at least 24 hours to make a decision and at least a few hours before a meeting is called to gather information that lets everyone contribute to the conversation."

Fifth, spell out both the positive and negative consequences of changing their approach.

"By giving me more time to make a decision, you can always count on me to give you 100% and supply with all the information you need to be successful. If I keep getting rushed into making decisions without adequate time or research, the projects will suffer from miscalculations, take longer than expected and cost the company more money than anticipated."

Sixth, make sure there's an agreement and invite the opportunity to clear up misunderstandings.

"Are we in agreement? Can we make this happen as of today?" or "Does that sound/seem/feel fair to you? Thank you."

16. If it's not your idea, then it's not worth looking at or implementing.

You have some great ideas. But an idea doesn't have to be yours to be a good one. In your relationships at work and home, the real shift occurs when you can listen to other people's ideas without making assumptions or prejudgments. You can always play devil's advocate – but questioning the pros and cons of an approach is different from shooting an idea down before it's even had the chance to be discussed.

This openness to idea generation matters, especially when it comes to brainstorming! Initially, you want to focus on quantity of ideas rather than the quality of those ideas. The first thought is seldom the best or most original or most profitable.

In an environment where more than one person contributes, ideas create a feeling of ownership. Soliciting ideas lets everyone feel part of the ultimate decision. Group solicitation dramatically increases the energy contributors invest to make sure that the final decision becomes a reality. Besides, your ability to act on an idea, or improve an approach is far more critical than originating it.

Before you toss another person's idea aside, ask them:

a. for some time to think about the concept or to let it incubate so that you (and everyone else) can form a meaningful response to the idea.

b. to submit a written plan of how they'd like to test, introduce or roll out the idea

c. to share the idea with a few additional individuals who can be objective and see, listen to and write down what they say.

17. You tend to interrupt questions or stop people in the middle of their comments.

In our efforts to streamline things and increase efficiencies it's important to remember that not everyone speaks, thinks or communicates as quickly as you!

Having to endure a conversation with a methodical or indirect or passive personality can be frustrating to be sure; Especially when you can almost see that word or phrase sitting on the tip of their tongue.

Still, interrupting or stopping others in the middle of their comments is often interpreted as rude, anti-social or indicative of poor upbringing.

Additionally, when you start trying to fill in their blanks, you end up shutting down your ability to genuinely comprehend the nuances of the information. You end up wasting everyone's time. You end up making costly mistakes too.

Rushing to conclusions leads to friction and missed opportunities because you seldom allow yourself to clearly and fully understand what a customer, coworker or manager was asking of you.

Recommendation?

Use the W.A.I.T Principle. Ask yourself, **Why Am I Talking?**

The best conversationalists are also the best listeners. Make a habit of talking less and listening more. Learn to let them speak up, even if it takes a bit longer to get to the point.

When you ask a question, do so without presuming the answer. Close your mouth and open your ears. Lean forward and keep your hands at your side to keep them from signaling to the speaker to speed up.

You should also start the conversation speaking at their rate, mirroring the inflections and pauses. Then, you can begin to model your faster pace and gradually increase your energy, intonation and body language so that they start to mirror you.

18. If it's not in your written job description, then it's not your responsibility.

Ideally, a written job description would list every possible task you might ever be expected to perform. This exhaustive list would remove any doubt about what is and isn't within your scope of responsibility. Employers often put three words somewhere towards the end of your job description – "Duties as Assigned." Maddening? Yes. Frustrating? Yes. The way things usually are? Yes!

The intent of #18 goes beyond the job description. What counts here is your willingness to contribute to the success of the people around you and ultimately, to the success of your organization and relationships at home. If you have some downtime, do you ask what else can be done to help out?

The more you contribute to the success of others the better off you are. Even if they (the people you volunteer to help) never reciprocate, you're still better off. Taking on responsibilities outside of your job description says a lot about your character. It demonstrates that you manage your time well.

It means that you are advanced enough to step outside of your comfort zone and look at a much broader picture that involves more than just your microcosm. It suggests that you are more promotable, more adaptable and are worth keep around when the next wave of job cuts hacks less valuable branches off the corporate tree.

You might be thinking or saying to yourself, "Why should I? They never help me. So what?"

Going beyond the basic expectation allows you to operate at a higher attitudinal frequency. You'll get your reward in ways you never imagined. If the powers that be rebuff your offer to take on additional responsibilities, that's okay too. Some people are going to be threatened by your proposal because they lack the insight of knowing that the only way to have power is to share power.

19. People should know what we expect of them, and what we're thinking. After all, it's their job!

You may be a highly intuitive person. If you're like me, you can sense a person's emotional state as soon as you walk into the same room with them. This intuition, although helpful, doesn't make us mind readers. Considering the rarity of intuition, is it fair to expect others to know what we need from them and what we're thinking? You know the answer, don't you?

Part of our jobs at home and work is to set and reinforce our expectations. With all the stuff a person needs to remember on a regular basis and all the conversations that happen daily, reminders make sense.

Plus, it's better to risk over communicating than to assume that other people have committed every detail of our 3-week old conversation to memory.

If someone is working for you, it is in their best interest to be frank with you by telling you when they don't know what to do, how to do it, why they should do it and how long they're expected to do it.

Your responsibility, in turn, is to practice empathy and give your contractor's, employee's and team member's feedback some consideration, even if you have a photographic memory and never forget anything.

Questions:

Am I communicating expectations in a variety of ways, explicitly leveraging as many mediums to assure the highest level of retention?

How did I communicate my last important request or idea? Did I write it down? Did I use graphs, charts or even PowerPoint? Did I share it by telephone? Did I share my message face-to-face?

Did I invite those in attendance to bring voice recorders?

Did I encourage the use of smartphones, laptops, pens, and pads of paper, or appoint an official transcriber to capture the conversation and my specific expectations?

Did I make a copy of my notes and give them to the person or group afterward?

If retention seems to be a more significant problem, what incentives can you introduce to encourage better listening, higher retention, and better implementation?

20. You have a right to yell at, insult and berate others, or physically assault them if they upset you or you don't get your way.

You were probably wondering whether this statement applied to home or work. The answer is both! I hope that you answer with an honest no to this one in both realms.

In the workplace, resorting to violence and anger is a surefire way to get fired. One of the foundations to a positive work environment is the understanding that it is a safe, non-hostile place, free from the fear of a person getting violent just because they get upset or they don't get their way.

Instead of getting violent with a person use these strategies:

1. Recommend a timeout. Say something like, "Let's take a 15-minute break. I need to walk away right now and be left alone. Please don't say another word. When we come back, we'll discuss this rationally." Then turn around and get away from the person you've let upset you.

2. Remember that in most cases, it's not personal and should not deteriorate into an attack on a person's character, their family or their private life. Focus on the person's behaviors and actions and ask them to do the same.

3. If something didn't go your way, keep your energies devoted to thinking logically. What role did the person in front of you personally play in your situation? Even if they are directly involved, are they just following established company protocol and following orders? Was it Murphy's Law? Are you the victim of an act beyond anyone's control?

4. Use the six-step assertiveness response outlined in statement #15.

Specify what you want to happen in the future and ask the parties to do what they can to "make it right."

5. If it's your fault then just shut up and listen attentively. If warranted, ask the other person if they want you to go into "listen only" mode or to go into "problem solve" mode. Don't interrupt or assume that you know what they're going to say. If the source of their anger still seems vague then ask for clarification. Restate or paraphrase what you think they said to you.

67

After they've had a chance to vent, it's time for you to apologize. "I'm sorry" goes a long way. Offer to fix the mess up or misunderstanding by emphasizing what you can do. Be specific about what and when you're going to fix or rectify the situation.

6. Keep your cool. A Chinese proverb teaches us that "If you are patient in one moment of anger, you will escape a hundred days of sorrow." Think about the long-term impact of your words and actions during a heated argument. Anger can rip a career or relationship to shreds in seconds. Is it worth losing everything?

7. Don't make promises you can't keep or demand assurances from others that they can't make legally or realistically due to real-life limitations. Know your boundaries, capabilities and slightly under promise with the intention of over delivery and exceeding their expectations.

8. Where appropriate, defuse the anger with a little humor. It's hard to laugh or smile and be angry at the same time. What's funny or humorous about the situation? What could have happened that would have made this case look like a non-event?

9. Ask the person exactly how he would like the problem resolved. Breathing slowly and deeply, ask questions like "If you were in my shoes and my position what would you do to resolve this?" or "What do suggest I do at this precise moment to fix this?"

21. You can't trust people to work (or do what you've asked them to do) without constant supervision.

People CAN be trusted to work without constant supervision – provided we've satisfied three criteria.

First, they're **trained** to work without constant supervision. Second, the person or team understands the **benefits** of working without constant supervision. Third, they know the **consequences** of proving to you that they can't be trusted to work without constant supervision.

Regardless of the role you're playing – parent, partner, manager, coworker, coach – you can only succeed if you can trust the people around you to do what they've agreed to do without you having to be the consummate babysitter, referee or jail warden.

Have a hard time walking away from the people you've asked to complete projects on your behalf? Get in a car and drive away. Turn off your smartphone, pager, wireless connection and anything else you might ordinarily use to keep tabs on your workers, friends and loved ones.

Ask yourself these questions:

Has the person(s) you've asked to do something received the most current training on the correct or optimal way to do the job?

Have you laid out the positive benefits of doing what you asked without you having to micromanage every part of the process? Positive benefits might include autonomy, respect, the chance to take on new challenges, trust, self-sufficiency, more opportunities to grow, the increased ability to decide where they work, who they work with, and openings to earn more money.

What are the specific negative consequences of NOT meeting the expectations?

Why can't I trust others to work without constant supervision?

Am I insecure about my work relationships?

Do my coworkers and staff trust me?

How do I know?

If they trusted me, what would I expect of them and how much harder would I work to maintain that trust?

22. The best results come through micro-managing the actions of every person involved in a project, task, team or activity.

See the comments on #21. The best results come when you can focus on the big picture and keep yourself from getting stuck doing the individual tasks that other people are better suited to tackle and resolve.

As a manager and leader, you get paid to get results through your people. You get paid to make bigger decisions that give people clarity and to maintain a work environment that allows your employees to flourish.

The core of your job as a manager and leader is to train employees, trust them to do what's asked or expected and step back to give them the space and autonomy they need. Train, Trust. Step back. It is a dance. Trust. Train. Step back. Repeat.

Feeling as though you need to micro-manage people may also be symptomatic of a more significant issue. Have you convinced yourself that your presence is mandatory? Has a sense of self-importance crept into your life? Could it be that what you justify as "attention to detail," or "making sure it's done right" is actually an attempt at self-preservation?

Is your effort to remain or be seen as relevant having the opposite effect on your career and your relationships? Might your trust issues be hindering your ability to lead your team and alienating the people you should depend on to get work done?

Additionally, giving your team, employees, coworkers and staff breathing room requires honest self-assessment; calling things what they are. You're not Mama Bear or Papa Bear; You're suffocating the people you claim to be protecting. You're not a protective analyst; you're letting conceit – and possibly your trust issues – rule your judgment.

23. The process is more important than the outcome.

Sometimes it is! Years of failures and successes often reveal best practices. Just keep in mind that best practice means it's the best practice at the moment and most systems can always be improved to get better outcomes.

The process may be as important as the outcome, especially when doing something in a specific order is critical to its success. For example, getting creative with the process of preparing a syringe to inject something into someone is a big no-no. Does it mean syringes are the **only or ultimate** delivery system? Of course not. Long-term, medicines that are absorbed instantly through the skin without needles or designing orally ingested medications are examples where a process can be improved to impact the outcome positively.

Or consider the process of hiring. There are specific questions to ask (or avoid) when interviewing a potential hire.

But do you have to ask the questions in a predetermined order?

Can the quality of the questions asked be improved?

How about the environment in which the questioning takes place?

At work, these current processes lead to systems that predictably create safe working conditions, optimal uses of marketing dollars, and fast completion of everyday tasks. It's all about finding a happy medium.

Balance your attention. At one end of managing, there's obsessing over the tiny things you do to complete a task or project. At the opposite end of managing, there's the mistake of giving your staff, colleagues, and teams zero direction, with zero regards to the structure or explicitly stating the desired outcome. Find the sweet spot between the two extremes.

When sharing your expectations with the people you work with give them latitude.

In fact you might say something like, "As long as your actions are ethical, safe, legal, fiscally responsible, documented, and on time, then do what you need to do to get the job done. Respect my stated outcome and the objectives the company has set, and I'll respect your right to be flexible with the established process. Fair enough?"

24. People should respect you because you've paid your dues.

This sentiment represents an aspect of Generational Privilege. It's code for "I'm older than you are and that mandates your fealty and respect."

The reality is this; The premise that someone owes you respect, opportunity, or a free pass because of what you've been through, or because an ancestor was slighted centuries ago is ridiculous. It's this kind of thinking that cements your feet in the past with little hope of ever moving forward.

People should respect you because you've **earned** their respect. While some people might admire you for the accomplishments you've reached through your life or even the hardships you've endured, those are hardly reasons to expect people to:

- respect you

- take your word as gospel

- or for them to remain silent while you remind them of how hard things were in the early days.

Our pasts do not predict our futures. And just because you paid your dues, it shouldn't mean others should have to pay the same price you did. It means your hard work and the lesson learned along the way hopefully made it more comfortable for the people walking in your footsteps to improve the processes they use and the outcomes they reach.

Questions:

What are you doing to earn the respect of the people who know you?

In what ways are you enhancing your level of respect through the decisions you make, the risks you take and the opportunities you create?

Do your actions mirror your words and can you demonstrate your competency when necessary?

Are you leveraging your status and authority to strengthen the loyalty people feel towards you? Or, are you abusing your status and power by resorting to threats, chest-beating, and banking on your former days of glory?

25. People should immediately respect you because of your life experiences.

Be sure to revisit my comments for statement #24. At this point, it's vital to add that while life experiences are more important than any formal degree you might earn, those past experiences don't translate into immediate respect. Respect is earned and based on transactions you make in the present, not the past.

The fact that you survived a war, or market crash, a troubled childhood, the loss of someone or something you care about, addiction, or spiritual crisis doesn't make you different. It makes you human. Welcome to life. What are you doing now, in the present moment to earn and keep a person's respect for you?

Questions:

How do your experiences help you to help others?

What have your past experiences taught you about life and what are you doing daily to be a coach and mentor when asked?

What have you done today to warrant the respect, trust and loyalty of the people you work with?

26. People should respect you because you're the boss and you've got the title to prove it.

Sure you're the boss. The title might get you an obligatory "good morning" or even get you a parking space. But it won't get you respect. In fact, holding the title of Boss or Master or Chief or Manager actually requires you to work **harder** to gain and retain the respect of the people who work with you.

People are going to be suspicious of you because your title pits you, a paid mouth, against them, the "overworked, underappreciated" masses. They'll hold you to a higher standard, watching you, looking for any reason to validate their innate suspicions that you are evil incarnate.

Only through consistency and congruency can you expect to earn and hold on to their respect. Respect is fragile and fleeting. Accept that reality. Resist the urge to assume that your title will do the heavy lifting on your behalf.

27. If it ain't broke, don't fix it.

This sentiment is a tough one to answer. Sometimes, it's wise not to break certain things because years of testing, validation, trial, and error have produced the best scenario, the best configuration, or the best arrangement (for the moment).

Other times, things are the way they are because the people involved are just too lazy, too ignorant, or too complacent to try to improve the "way it's always been done."

Systems and rituals have their place. They help us make sense of things and help others to learn best practices quickly and consistently. They provide guidance and direction, especially in complicated situations where specificity or order is crucial.

Sometimes, shortcutting the process destroys or diminishes the intended outcome. The journey facilitates learning and provides a connection to the group.

When it comes to tinkering with what's working, perhaps the best questions to ask are:

"What could happen if we break it and can't make it work again?"

"What's the absolute worst that could happen if we changed the boundaries?"

"What are the consequences of doing nothing?"

For instance, what happens if we change the boundaries of our existing business relationship to include new vendors?

What's the worst that could happen by tweaking the "recipe" or process we follow to get to the finished product or service? What's the best that could happen?

If we do nothing are we strong enough to survive the changing marketplace?

If we just keep doing what we are doing will our relationships with customers or clients strengthen or evaporate?

28. Other people always have stupid ideas that would never work and aren't worth your attention.

Be wary of using words like "always" and "never." These words often paint you into a dead end. Few things really are "never" and "always" so be selective about the things you apply them to. Speaking in such absolutes – primarily as they relate to ideas and the issues that people bring up – shuts down the exchange of information.

Assuming in advance that the opinions and alternatives you will hear or read about are in some way inferior to your own creates the perception that you are a somewhat pompous individual. People of character welcome ideas contrary to their own and use the exchange to tweak and re-evaluate their current positions.

Perceptions aside, when you enter a conversation from the perspective that other peoples ideas are worthless you annihilate the very environment that needs to exist. Specifically, you block idea exchanges, debates, and brainstorming that can lead to real progress. Your skeptical, negative verbal, and non-verbal language also discourages the sense of connection and trust that must exist for business and personal relationships to thrive.

To be fair, not every idea anyone comes up with is necessarily brilliant. In business, propositions need to make or save money. In other areas, a plan must achieve something tangible as well; saving time or money, building relationships, creating simplicity, peace of mind, confidence, loyalty, or saving lives.

If someone takes the initiative to share an idea, it's worthy of some consideration. Ask the person making suggestions to share their concept clearly, using their most potent mode of communication (pictures, words, print, spoken, paper, screen, etc.). It's also fair to ask them to back up their ideas with facts, research and details. When someone shares an idea, acknowledge it. Thank them. Then, ask for follow-up.

Show the person presenting the idea that you are listening. Force yourself to consider the merit of the ideas by engaging, acknowledging and questioning.

"Okay, I hear what you're saying. How would we make it happen?"

"What are some of the logistics that would go into making sure the idea works?"

"How would we know that the idea was successful?"

"What are some measurable metrics that we could look at so that we could evaluate the effectiveness of the idea and whether the time and energy and resources allocated to the idea were worthwhile?"

Besides, coming up with and sharing at least SOME ideas is often better than no ideas. Informed thought leads to informed results. Plus, plenty of bizarre ideas have led to some huge windfalls. The Pet Rock. Plastic Wishbones. Post-it Notes. The personal computer. Fidget spinners.

If you're the type of person who prefers to see things written down, then say so. Also, there's no mandate that you have to approve or shoot down an idea the moment it's presented. Instead, ask for time to consider the idea and get back to the originator later.

29. Spontaneity is foolish.

This statement warrants a definite sometimes. It depends on the consequences that spontaneity may create.

If, for example, you see an email advertising a software upgrade that would help the department but is expensive or hasn't been approved for purchase in advance, you might be best served to squelch spontaneity (since the money isn't yours to spend).

If you're tempted to stop at the casino on the drive home (and you can't afford to lose the $100 you want to gamble with), then being spontaneous is going to be hurtful.

Since spontaneity is mostly situational, the starting point for many spontaneous decisions begins with questions like:

Who gets hurt if I do this?

What are the potential consequences (both positive and negative) of my actions?

What do I (or the people who I am responsible to) benefit from most? The immediate gratification of being able to be spontaneous? Or the long-term benefit of demonstrating discipline by saying no?

You should be able to process these questions reasonably quickly without obsessing over whether you've made a wise decision.

Additionally, you always have the right to ask others for their assistance in making a decision. The trick here is finding someone who can advise you without bias.

Who can you ask for a second opinion who has no vested interest in you making a quick decision?

You're **not** going to ask the car salesperson if you should buy the car or ask the travel agent if you should book an impromptu weekend getaway. You're **not** going to ask the person who wants your job if you should quit.

In these examples, the clear bias of the person wanting you to make a decision dilutes the value of their opinion that you should act impulsively.

In all situations, step back and ask the above questions. Who gets hurt? What are the potential positive and negative consequences of my decisions? Can I deal with those consequences? Do I benefit most from being spontaneous or by waiting?

The answers will help you to make the best spontaneous decision every time.

If you can't come to a fast decision (and the situation indeed requires an immediate response), give yourself another few minutes to weigh the pros and cons.

Spontaneity can recharge us and change our lives for the better forever. Or it can lead to years or a lifetime of regret. Perhaps a good mantra is "Spontaneity in moderation."

30. Before presenting an idea, you must plan every word you're going to say and stick to it, no matter what.

Yes, you should spend time planning how you want to present an idea. Yes, you want to map out a logical flow of facts and combine them with relevant stories and examples to support those points. You should also spend time anticipating the potential rebuttals the person or people you speak to will use to test, reject or deflect your ideas. You may even practice word for word, writing out and vocalizing what you want to say.

That said, life is not a scripted story. You seldom have the luxury of being able to control all aspects of an event (be it a meeting, a press conference, speech, an intervention with a family member, colleague, employer or employee).

You have to walk into any situation knowing that despite your most meticulous planning and expectation of what you were going to say, the environment you envisioned will not materialize.

What happens if your window of opportunity to speak doesn't materialize at the moment you thought it would?

What happens if your allotted time to speak suddenly drops to half?

What if you learn some last minute news that either helps or hurts your position on an issue?

The point is, you've got to be flexible and remain relaxed enough to change what you say and how you say it at a moment's notice. No one knows what you left out or forget to mention.

Don't be so scripted or rehearsed that you can't adapt or respond to a change in the plan on the fly. Freezing up weakens your ability to get what you want.

It's up to you to create the opportunity to speak up and share your thoughts. When you've created the moment, use it to say what needs to be said, even if it's not under the circumstances you imagined.

If delivering your message in person doesn't work out, consider the various methods you can use to share ideas.

Can you write your words down and present them as an email, as an op-ed piece, as a blog entry, as a memo, or as a formal letter or proposal?

Can you video tape yourself and send the message in the mail on a DVD or jump drive?

Can you upload your video to YouTube or Facebook?

Can you record your words and share them via phone, as a podcast, or as an MP3 file?

Can you merge your words with pictures via PowerPoint or just use photographs with headlines and forego words altogether?

31. If a task has not been entered into your daily calendar or on your to-do list, then you won't do it.

Having the discipline to create a daily or monthly to-do list is admirable and necessary, especially since time is a rare commodity for most of us.

The higher up the corporate ladder you climb, the more you'll be expected to juggle multiple meetings and multiple tasks. Many of my friends in executive positions or project managers have their entire day mapped out before they get to work. It's one meeting, planning session, project review, budget decision, resource or vendor discussion after another.

At home, your role as spouse, lover, parent, friend, pet owner, bill payer, remodeler, coach, taxi driver, shopper, and therapist requires informed choices in how and where you spend your time and how you prioritize what gets done.

With so many things to do and so little productive time to do them, it makes sense to map out your day, your week and the next few months of your life.

Additionally, having a legitimate to-do list prevents time-stealers and people who are too lazy to do their work from saddling you with projects you can't (or shouldn't) reasonably take on. As you've probably discovered, some people will delegate responsibility all day long if allowed! Having your list of priorities is a good deterrent from being saddled with someone else's

Ask yourself the following.

Are you a prisoner to your daily calendar and to-do list?

You know you're a prisoner when 1) you are unable to respond to an unplanned event or relevant request from a loved one, peer or co-worker. And 2) when you lack the mental or physical strength to pull away from your schedule long enough to make a decision or provide feedback or recognize others for their contributions, talents or accomplishments.

When the thought of deviating from your agenda paralyzes you, you run the risk of being rolled over by the randomness of life.

Are you using your calendar as an excuse to avoid helping others (when in reality, you have the time)?

There's a difference between being legitimately busy and just saying you're working to avoid helping others.

When you're consistently unavailable (while it's painfully apparent that you have capacity) you alienate others and force them to look elsewhere for answers. This construct creates a physical and emotional disconnect that weakens your relationships. You demonstrate via your unavailability that you're potentially replaceable and unnecessary to the continuity of a project or department.

Furthermore, rigidity is not endearing! A little compromise to your schedule helps your relationships and facilitates positive reciprocity. The chaos of life circumvents the best-laid plans.

Your willingness to depart from the script (when necessary) to assist others and provide support makes a huge difference in every area of your life.

32. Asking for assistance from others is a sign of weakness.

Asking for assistance from others is a sign of strength, humility and exceptional character.

While you should be able to complete the majority of your work based on the skill sets, expertise, and experience that you possess, few things can be accomplished entirely alone.

We live in a complex world; one that requires input from as many informed sources as is practical. Reaching out to the owners of proprietary information and those with access to knowledge beyond your own makes sense.

Attempting to do big things without plugging into a support network is akin to insanity. You'll find that even those things which you can complete alone may often be accomplished faster, less expensively and more accurately when you include others.

The caveat here is that you turn to the right people for support.

Who is qualified to give you an informed opinion and meaningful direction?

Who can you trust to be honest with you and not subvert information that you might need?

Answer these questions first, and you'll save time and headache.

Before you ask for help, spell out your questions so that you respect the time of the person or group. Be as precise as possible and be ready to show preliminary research you've already conducted, as well as potential solutions you've considered.

If you don't know, say so. Reach out to people who do know, or to people who can put you in touch with people who know.

Conversely, when a person comes to you asking for assistance, don't automatically shoo them away or let your ego get the best of you. It takes a lot of strength to admit your limitations. Put yourself in their position and treat them with the level of professionalism, respect, and candidness you'd expect if the roles were reversed.

33. If someone doesn't agree with you, then that person has a severe mental problem.

The nerve of some people! How dare they disagree with you? Don't they know who you are? Surely they must be crazy, delusional, and inferior to you; Unworthy to be in your presence!

But seriously, mental health is not something to take lightly. Throwing words around like "crazy" or "delusional" might be closer to the truth than someone is comfortable joking about.

Rather than pinning a person's disagreement on their mental state, it's better to embrace the reality that expecting others to agree with you blindly is small-minded, self-opinionated and dangerous.

It's small-minded because everyone walks a unique path formed by thousands of decisions and thousands of events. Unless you've walked precisely on the same road, you can't reasonably expect someone to think as you do; at least not all the time. **Besides, any firmly held conviction is worthy of scrutiny.**

Additionally, you don't know what you don't know. Your goal should not be to have others continuously agree with you without merit. Instead, your goal is to learn to articulate your ideas powerfully with the understanding that they may never be universally accepted.

Attack the idea, not the person. A debate is an efficient way to keep dogmatic thinking from suffocating your creativity and keep you from getting stuck in one place.

Think about your thoughts. What makes you right? Would you believe what you do even if no one else held the same opinion?

Even if you are right, accept that it may take a lifetime for others to see your perspective as gospel. In the meantime, document why you believe as you do. More importantly, model your ideas through your actions. Let your truth guide you. Use your beliefs to create personal meaning and purpose without usurping the rights of others to think differently.

To avoid becoming a stick in the mud, you must continuously seek out differences of opinion, even if the views you encounter are in stark contrast to your own. If someone doesn't agree with you – and is honest enough to say so – welcome them into your inner circle of advisers. Applaud the right of other to hold positions contrary to your own. Leverage their candidness to keep you sharp. Value truthfulness over benign consensus.

Surrounding yourself with clones of you is a bad idea. Even worse is expecting others to rubber stamp your beliefs and accept your words as inerrant. If you encounter a yes man or yes person, ask them why they agree with you. Is it blind faith or a well thought out conclusion based on individual contemplation or research?

In the end, you can also agree to disagree.

34. Your winning personality is all you need to get by in any situation.

There can be no denying. A winning personality will take you places! Looking your best and working on your ability to interact confidently, positively and authentically with others should be at the top of your personal development list. An authentic kindness, respect and genuine interest in others will take you farther than bullying your way through life.

Still, you need to know your facts. While a winning personality beats out the dry academics some of the time, looks and wit alone will not be sufficient in all matters. A great smile and charm are merely a foot in the door, not the end-all-be-all. Don't let vanity blind you to the need to be more than just a pretty face or possess a charming disposition. The more you can offer in the way of practical know-how, the better.

For example in every team dynamic, whether it's a group of two or twenty, there has to be someone who assumes one or more of the following roles:

Visionary; the person with a big picture perspective of what needs to happen

Verbalizer; the person who can convey that vision to others meaningfully through words, pictures and stories

Actualizer; the person who has the tenacity to see the project through and get things done

Detailer; the person who can take the big picture and the words and identify the myriad small things that need to happen to get the job done legally, within budget and on-time

Equalizer; the person who can keep the rest of the people on the team focused and help mitigate potential communication breakdowns or personality clashes.

More than personality, each of these roles requires core competencies that are unique yet critical to the resolution of the task, scenario or project at hand.

Which of these functions would you be able to assume?

What can your experience and insights contribute to the work or situation at hand?

Whatever your skill set, don't be lazy. Contribute to the team. Share ideas. Use your brain. Articulate your thoughts and be prepared to defend them. Participate by rolling your sleeves up and offering solutions. Take on the role that suits you and perform it to the absolute best of your ability.

35. It's all about facts. People should agree with you because you know more than they do. You've got the degree, certification, and experience to prove it.

As discussed in the previous statement, personality plays a vital role in the art of getting what you want. Sure, you may have the technical proficiency and the years of schooling or decades of experience to support your claims. But if you're a jerk or tyrant or arrogant in how you present yourself and your demands, the road to buy-in is slow and painful.

What matters is not **what** you know but **how** you present what you know. You must package your facts in a way that conveys your opinion understandably and concisely.

You also have to show those who you want to agree with you how they benefit from your approach or how your ideas are in some way an extension of their current positions.

Experience and educational merits are never valid reasons to be pompous or condescending towards others. Are you considerate of others? Are you able to adapt your communication style to complement the communication style of those you wish to persuade?

Not everyone thinks, acts or processes information like you do. Expecting them to do so, especially from the position of factual superiority, is actually naïve, haughty and a sure way to turn people off for good.

You can be honest without being rude. You can convey ideas without being smug. Unless you can infuse your facts and knowledge with humility and humanity, you're best to keep your opinions to yourself.

Before trying to cram ideas down someone's throat or demanding buy-in from others, begin the process with empathy. See the world from their perspective. Understand the foundation of their current values, culture and belief systems.

Facts, coupled with tact and heart-to-heart connections will earn you the respect of those around you and open their minds to the possibility that your ways may be better.

36. There's a place for everything, and everything should be in its place.

Most of the time, this one earns an emphatic YES! The people you work with and live with have a right to expect shared items to be readily available and accessible.

Things like tools, keys, remotes, frequently used documents, music and picture files, and devices should have a designated space. Filing a paid invoice, or entering a phone number or storing an email in the right location is hardly an unfair expectation.

Having a specific place to put something is foundational to creating a successful system. Successful systems drive successful businesses. They also make life more efficient and less stressful.

More importantly, following a place for everything and everything in its place principle makes getting along with others more likely. Who enjoys repeatedly asking or hearing "Where is it?" or Where do you put the...?" or "Has anyone seen the...?"

We waste so much time searching for misfiled, misplaced stuff or searching for stuff thrown into indiscriminate piles. It's time that could have been used for real work, improving your work environment or extended leisure.

A messy desk is not a sign of genius. It's a sign of someone with a dangerously short attention span with hoarder tendencies. It's a sign of someone who likes to re-invent the wheel almost daily, wasting considerable time in the process.

Challenges:

Pick a single spot to hang your keys and go an entire week putting the keys in that location. No exceptions.

Then pick a few items at work that you use every day. Pick a spot on your desk or a specific drawer and make that space the "official" place for that item.

37. We should avoid change because things are fine just the way they are.

This may warrant a sometimes. Some things really are good the way they are. Consistency and familiarity make us comfortable. This truism explains why we like our traditions and rituals; they often create an anchor that we can hold on to in a world where relationships and principles break apart and drift away with little warning.

We work hard to create an environment where customers and employees know what to expect day in and day out. The rules and expectations we follow often help to define our roles and boundaries. When those rules and expectations change abruptly, the resulting chaos can be painful for everyone involved.

Despite the feel-good associations and certainty that comes with rituals, systems, rules and familiar expectations, change happens whether you like it or not. At work and home, things change regularly. People. Technologies. Goals and priorities.

With new information, we are expected to reevaluate the rituals and ideologies we hold sacred. With unique insights and experiences, we are supposed to become a better version of our previous self.

Then there's the brute force approach. With enough might, change can be slowed – temporarily. Still, the forbidden whispers of dissent and the civil debates or protests silenced now are the violent coups, life-changing revolutions and mass extinctions of tomorrow. Whether it's now or later, change will come, and seldom on your terms.

Rather than fighting change, expect it. Flow with it so that you don't get mired in the clay. Anticipate that things will change. Stay ahead of the change by challenging yourself to innovate on a regular basis. Ask yourself and the people you cherish what you need to do to benefit from the impending cycle of change. Will it be new skills? Updated beliefs? Newfound courage? Transparency and honesty?

Life is better with your eyes wide open.

38. Why can't things be like the good old days?

The good old days? One of the few things worse than using past events (mean parents, lack of education, born on the wrong side of the tracks, poorly-chosen employers, etc.) to rationalize our current circumstances, is using the past to minimize the value of the present.

It's easy to wax nostalgic about the past, especially as the days turn into years and years turn into decades. It is also easy to crave consistency that the past might seem to represent, mainly when it seems the world beneath our feet drops away by the second.

The past can be a warm blanket that warms us against the winds of change, doubt, and uncertainty. The memories and wisdom of those we loved but who are now departed comforts us.

If we are fast learners and not gluttons for punishment, the lessons of the past help us to avoid repeating atrocities and outright stupid decisions.

The problem lies in over-relying on the past and turning to it as a permanent reprieve from the present. By continually using the past as a sort of gold standard, that warm blanket quickly turns into a prison.

Those memories of yesterday – often embroidered and filtered through a siphon of wishful thinking – can suck the winds of innovation and possibility out of the room and our life. Yearning for the good old days can make the most motivated among us apathetic and joyless.

And that's not all. Using the past to vilify the present prevents us (and the people around us) from enjoying **this moment**. This moment is what matters. What you do and say, and how you choose to interact with the people and events that occur in the minutes and hours ahead is the only thing you can control or influence with any certainty.

Yearning for the days of old is exhausting and leads to a dead end. The good old days – which weren't necessarily always good – are gone.

Consider a better use of the energy you pour into hoping:

That your favorite sports team was still around.

Or that you had less responsibility.

Or that times were more straightforward.

Or that you were single again.

Or that so and so was still president.

Or that your neighbors were people who looked and acted like you.

That energy can be better spent improving yourself, connecting with the people you cherish and creating events worth remembering.

The good old days will seldom be better than the "good-todays." Not every day is perfect or free of stress and frustration. Still, today is better than yesterday. Why? Because we have access to more solutions, more rights, more choices, more options, and more alternatives. We have more room to disagree. We have more say in how we connect, how we communicate, and how we decide to pursue our career and our calling(s).

Your past successes are precisely that; past successes. Fortunately, so are your past failures. They're in the past. They're history. So let go and move forward with your life!

39. It's not your job to ask questions. If people have a problem, they'll tell you about it.

If you don't ask then who will? In a room full of 10 professionals, at least eight of them are confused as to what's being discussed. But, they stay quiet, shaking their heads up and down, pretending to agree with or understand what is being said by you or whoever else is speaking.

Why? Because they're scared of looking dumb. And they figure that someone else will raise their hand or be bold enough to ask the burning question.

Unfortunately, no one does.

Under-communicating is the reason so many projects fail to be completed on time or budget. Assuming that others understand you the first time around is dangerous. It puts relationships at risk and futures in jeopardy.

Don't rationalize or live in the land of "shouldas" (He shoulda asked. She shoulda said something.) Instead, adopt the position that it IS your job to ask questions and to clarify your position and expectations.

Use every means possible to give the people you work with an outlet to express their apprehensions or misgivings upfront.

Ask questions that help people to "come clean" about the challenges or roadblocks they face along the way. When in doubt ask the simple question, "Am I making sense?" and wait for a verbal response.

If you suspect that people are just nodding and not really getting you, follow up with,

"What part of what I'm saying do you agree with the most?"

"Why do you agree or disagree with me on this?"

"Who can tell me what this (diagram, word, phrase, item, etc.) means?"

"Who else should we be having this conversation with?"

"What, about what I've just said, do you have questions on?"

"What will it take to (roll this out, finance this, make this happen, fix it, complete this project)?

"What's the next step then?"

"When can I expect you to get back to me with a plan?"

"Just in case, what do you suggest we go with as Plan B?"

Verify that the people around you know:

    -precise expectations,

    -who is responsible for what

    -and have ample opportunities to solicit suggestions from people who might have the knowledge you seek.

Courageous people ask questions. They admit when they don't know something. They ask questions to clarify their understanding and to help others see the problem through multiple lenses.

If you're in a situation where someone else is speaking, (and you don't get it, and you sense that others are not getting it either) calmly say, "I'm not sure if it's just me, but I am not following what you're saying. Could you back up and explain what you mean by....?"

As you speak, address precisely what you don't understand. When asking your question or seeking clarity, focus on what's being said versus focusing on the skills or personality of who is speaking.

Remember that questioning is the DNA of innovation, discovery, and revelation. Regardless of your position or station in life, you should ask questions and seek to understand as often as possible. Even when scorned by others for asking them, good questions yield good answers and dismantle time bombs before they detonate.

Good answers also lead to shared goals and consensus. Shared goals bring people together who in turn build great systems and solve problems in less time with less redundancy. Great systems provide peace of mind and free us up to focus on our bigger dreams and aspirations. Peace of mind and the freedom to dream are priceless rewards for those who dare to ask why.

40. If people dedicate themselves to their jobs, then they don't need on-going incentives or motivation.

Why do people dedicate themselves to a job in the first place? A dedicated person immerses themselves into whatever they are doing because they want to do an excellent job. They want to give 100%. They want to solve problems, help people and move a project forward. That person wants to feel that their contributions to a plan or workplace have made a positive, tangible difference.

But the moment arrives in virtually every job or long-term project when you begin to wonder if your skills and talents matter. Are you just a warm body? The daily grind and daily routines start to cloud the original reason you started working in your position in the first place. The finish line gets moved further away. The specs change so much that you and the people you work with become disillusioned.

Worse yet, negativity starts to creep in. "Why am I working so hard in the first place?" "Why am I wasting my time when nothing ever gets done or improved anyway?" "Anyone can do my job. I'm just another cog in the machine."

People remain dedicated when they know that their contributions matter.

Here's the thing. How do the people you work with know if they are viewed as an asset and valued for their skills and knowledge?

The most potent incentive you can provide to anyone is informed feedback. We want to know how we are doing. Assuming that your opinion is valued, unbiased and sincere, your honest feedback can keep the most distraught employee moving forward.

This effect remains even when the feedback isn't full of glowing accolades and smiley faces. That said, letting people know what they are doing well is just as important as letting people know what they are doing poorly. The need for positive feedback is especially real in an environment where employees get chastised for doing things incorrectly more than they receive praise for doing things exceptionally well.

You might argue that a regular paycheck and not being fired at the end of the day are adequate feedback tools. While the prospect of consistently earning money creates a financial incentive, there are lots of ways to make money. You and the people you work with have choices about:

- who they work for,

- where they work,

- and how long they work there.

Money isn't everything. Our search for meaning extends into our workplace, and we want to know where we fit into the ecosystem. That's why it's essential to offer your employees, vendors, contractors and service providers feedback on how they are doing.

Dedication wanes in the absence of guidance, feedback, mentoring, encouragement, incentives and motivation. If you are the type of person who can do your job day in and day out without any input or reassurance, then you may make an excellent entrepreneur. Still, even those with rock-solid work ethics need to hear they are appreciated from time to time. If all else fails, remember this. A simple, sincere, in-person thank you goes a long way.

Regarding motivation, implementing employee of the month competitions, offering prized parking spots, and running various contests are short-term (and arguably hazardous) ways to boost morale. There are only two ways to motivate people consistently.

First, show people you trust them. That means giving employees autonomy. Micromanagement is the antithesis of trust. You also demonstrate your confidence in employees by giving them more significant responsibilities, inviting them to sit in on high-level discussions with top executives to provide feedback and share ideas, and giving them the green light to implement their vetted solutions to improving the workplace.

The second way to motivate consistently is to build reliable systems. Be passionate about creating and incrementally improving how things get accomplished.

When you can teach and pass on clear systems (ways of doing things) that produce measurable, reliable outcomes – especially those that don't require managers to hover constantly or need consultants from the outside to interpret – you reduce turnover and increase morale. Employees thrive in environments where they can be trained to use systems that are sustainable, congruent, duplicable, adaptable and result driven.

Is it Really Me? Is it My Work?

If the results of the STICK Survey leave you perplexed, consider the following:

1) Taken in a non-work context, your answers to many of the statements and scenarios might be different.

Who you are at work and who you are home are two very different personas. We become the darkest versions of ourselves when we feel cornered, stuck, out of control, and limited by the options we have to improve our situation.

Go through the STICK Survey again. This time, substitute words like "co-worker", "employee", "customer", "boss", "manager", "crew chief", "team lead", "vendor", or "competitor" with the names of your kids, your parents, your partners or spouse, your friends, and family and see what your totals reveal. If you receive the same score, then maybe it's time to work on yourself.

Be aware of the impact your words and actions have on others. Strive to become less self-centered and more people-centered. Be less focused on preserving your "kingdom" and more steadfast about following through, helping others to succeed, and taking responsibility for what happens under your watch. Accept feedback. Listen. Stay humble and be modest. In a few months retake the Stick Survey, and see how you do.

2) Maybe your score indicates that it is time for a change at work so that you can be that person you used to be.

If you've determined that your environment is turning you into a monster here's what you do.

Plan for changes so that you have options. Take an honest inventory of other skill sets you possess. Ask yourself "What else can I do?" even if it requires working in a completely different industry or career.

If you want to move somewhere else within the same company, then talk to your immediate supervisor and ask about opportunities for cross-training in other areas or departments. Seek out additional training either provided by your current employer or offered by a local college or online course.

Is your job in danger of being eliminated?

Pouting and complaining may delay the inevitable. But in the end, your position will be erased, probably permanently. Instead of closing your eyes and hoping for divine intervention or a last-minute reprieve, act decisively.

Talk to the person in your company responsible for jobs and let them know that despite the elimination of your current position, you'd like to stay with the company in a different role, location or department.

Ask the HR Director or manager what skills you'll need for this to happen. The fact is, as a current employee, you save the company money because they won't have to spend as much training you since you are familiar with the company culture, hierarchy, processes and politics.

Is it just time to find employment elsewhere?

If staying in your current company is not possible, do the following action steps. This checklist will make help make the change less painful and increase the odds of finding a job where you can start fresh.

___ Spend a few hours developing a kick-butt resume that highlights your real-world experience, your additional skill sets, and expertise. Haven't a clue what a resume should look like? Visit a local bookstore. Peruse resume books written in the last year or two and get ideas on the best ways to present yourself on paper and the web.

You'll find that "Objectives" are rather passé. Your resume is a marketing piece and nothing more. Still, the resume separates you from the dozens or hundreds of other applicants. It says to the employer "I am worth hiring… and here's why." It's a foot in the door to get an interview. The real work comes when you interview by phone or in person.

___ Go to job boards, look for jobs that seem appealing, copy the exact language used by the potential employer and paste their words into a customized resume that essentially parrots back the precise language they used in their job description. Wrap your experiences into a summary of qualifications that demonstrates – as realistically and honestly as possible – that you are the right person for that position.

___ Craft a one-page cover sheet, tailored for the job you want. The cover sheet succinctly presents your experiences and answers the question that universal question, "What will I get if I hire you?"

___ Practice interviewing, taking notice of your body language and nonverbal cues. Listen to the tone of your voice. Do you sound enthused or apathetic? Do you sound human or mechanical?

___ Come up with the most stringent questions you can imagine an interviewer asking you and develop cogent answers.

___ Research the company you want to interview at. Jot down questions you might have for the interviewer, and bring a notepad and pen to take notes.

___ Apply for the job. Be sure the cover sheet mentions the company and job title by name, along with a factoid that you feel is interesting or relevant to the position.

___ Follow up after a week (by email or by phone), asking to speak directly with the person responsible for hiring or arranging interviews.

___ If you hear nothing, move on. Use the template you've developed for your customized resume (which can be as long as necessary) and your cover sheet and market yourself to other companies looking for someone with your expertise.

___ Tweak your resume. Post your resume in every relevant place, both on and offline. Ask your friends and online network of associates to keep their eyes and ears open and to introduce you to people who might move you closer to a new position.

Whatever you do, don't get dismayed. Learn to be comfortable being uncomfortable. Keep in mind that when it comes to job searching, every NO is one step closer to YES.

CONCLUSION

Your beliefs about people and yourself influence the results you get and the relationships you foster. When you take the time to review your attitudes you mitigate the likelihood of becoming a liability to your organization.

Additionally, you want to remain in control of where you work, how long you stay, your scope of responsibilities, the projects you get to work on, and how you transition out when the time comes.

For these things to stay within your control, you have to audit your beliefs regularly and tweak those that might be weakening your options (and causing people to dread being around you).

You likely work with a person or two who has overstayed their welcome. But to everyone's detriment, that problem employee can't be fired or let go (union, contracts, seniority, no applicants to replace them at the salary offered). They often can't quit either because, understandably, they need to hold on to benefits like health insurance.

As you discovered taking the STICK Survey, many of these same people are too stuck to move. Their beliefs about life – and consequently, the way they treat others – have made them too toxic to hire or transfer anywhere else.

The astute person seeks to avoid getting locked in a negative pattern of self-preservation. It's a pattern that includes:

- blaming others

- hiding mistakes

- refusing to accept responsibility for errors

- criticizing others or creating false emergencies to shift attention away from performance issues

- engaging in gossip

- relying on personality to cover up product knowledge issues

- insisting on superiority and delusions of self-importance

- and participating in stick up your butt behaviors.

Even worse, a person's bitterness about being stuck in place is palpable. In the end, everyone suffers. Talented people leave when toxic people stay. When all that remains are toxic people, the organization's future dims. Customers seek out other product or service providers to avoid dealing with individuals in your company with a history of being too proud to improve and being too unreliable to "get it right" when it counts.

Employees want leaders who are confident (without being cocky), competent (without being compelled to micro-manage), consistent and predictable (without being overly wedded to negative beliefs or outmoded ways of doing things).

Leaders want employees who are committed, capable, coachable, competent and flexible.

Everyone wants people who can remain humble, honest, communicative, selfless, unassuming, accessible, positive, proactive, inclusive, broad-minded and sincere.

As the workplace continues to diversify, those who demonstrate the ability to grow into the next set of expectations will find the longevity, recognition, and freedom they crave.

Growth demands that you remain fluid in how you interact with co-workers, bosses, vendors, and customers. This fluidity is your most specific antidote to the threat of automation and global competition.

THANK YOU!

Thank you for reading *Too Stuck to Move*. The author hopes that you have found the ideas and suggestions helpful and applicable to your situation.

His sincere desire is that you take away some of the recommendations and implement a personal action plan so that you have higher job satisfaction, a renewed feeling of choice and flexibility in your job, and your life in general.

Perhaps you know a few people who might benefit from reading this book and taking the STICK Survey as well. **Please tell those individuals about this book**. Would you take a few moments to **write a review on Amazon or suggest this book to your local bookstore owner?**

While you're there, consider getting a few copies to lend to the people at work. Give the gift of self-awareness.

Brien Norris is also the author of *Problem Solving & Overcoming Obstacles: Transform Moments of Despair INTO Joy, Clarity, Healthy Self-Esteem, Contentment and Peace of Mind*

Questions? Comments? Feel free to email the author at BrienNorris1@gmail.com.

DEFINITIONS

Arrogant: Someone who acts excessively confident.

OPPOSITE: Modest

Blameshifter: To blame others for your failures or to refuse to take ownership of the outcomes of your decisions; To resist accountability and responsibility.

Conceited: Someone with an attitude or behavior that flaunts their intelligence, skills, or attractiveness.

OPPOSITE: Humility

Condescending: The behavior of someone who shows they think they are more important or more intelligent than other people.

OPPOSITE: Respectful

Egocentric: People who behave as if they are more important than others, and need not care anyone but themselves.

OPPOSITE: Selfless

Generational Privilege: Expecting preferred status, access, mobility, exceptions, and opportunities based on your age or the era in which you were born and the conditions that existed when you grew up. Common symptoms include demanding respect that you haven't earned, expecting praise you haven't done anything exceptional to receive and demanding income or promotions based on your age versus your talent or capabilities.

Haughty: Unbearably proud and high-minded; so overbearing in how a person presents themselves in words, mannerism, inflection, and actions that they practically reek of self-exultation.

OPPOSITE: Unassuming

Immodest: Someone who thinks that they are very good or smart and likes to talk about their achievements.

OPPOSITE: Modest (humble and unpretentious)

Narcissist: People with an extreme interest in their own lives and problems, preventing them from caring about other people.

OPPOSITE: Unselfish, empathetic

Patronizing: Behaving or speaking to others in a way that shows you think you are more intelligent or talented than they are.

OPPOSITE: Sincerity, inclusive, mature

Passive-aggressive: A type of behavior or personality identified by the use of covert actions to express disagreement and resistance indirectly.

A person who is passive-aggressive has issues about telling people how they feel about what someone asks of them. They often dislike or question the authority of the person making the demand, or resent the nature of the request or an expected action assigned to them.

Rather than saying no to the order, or asking for more information or getting to the why of the matter and expressing reservations or concerns, the passive-aggressive person resorts to using people, places, and things to create obstacles.

In their aversion to confrontation, a passive-aggressive person employs procrastinating, pouting, vague language, or misplacing project-specific materials or misdirecting vital information as a means to illustrating their real feelings.

OPPOSITE: Being openly and actively aggressive, forthright and direct. In the workplace, aggressive behavior gets a bad reputation. So, we employ **assertiveness** as a healthy alternative.

Self-importance: Conveying a belief that you are more important or valuable than others.

OPPOSITE: Unconceited, humility, egoless

Self-opinionated: Acting as though your own opinions are unquestionably correct and that everyone else should agree with you.

OPPOSITE: Uncomplacent, modest, broad-minded

Self-satisfied: Going on about how happy or fortunate you are about your station or status in life in a way that leads others to conclude that you hold too high an opinion of yourself.

OPPOSITE: Egoless

Stick up Your Butt: An umbrella term that refers to a person who is easily offended, considered repressive, rigid, unjustifiably formal, overly focused on protocol and the "right" way to do something.

Someone with a "stick up the butt" is seen as humorless, robotic, inflexible (to the detriment of others), pompous, unpleasant to be around, and irritable. They use anger to control, intimidate, or deflect attention away from their shortcomings.

They complain about unimportant things, whine, assume the worst and often suck the creativity and joy out of a room merely by being present. They tend to be unjustifiably stern, paternalistic, authoritarian and prone to highlighting failure instead of acknowledging accomplishments.

Snobbery: Attitudes or behavior that suggests a person is better than other people. A snob gives off an offensive air of superiority and tends to ignore or disdain anyone regarded as inferior.

OPPOSITE: Humility

Superior: Someone who behaves as though they are better or more important than other people.

OPPOSITE: Anti-elitist, egalitarian (relating to or believing in the principle that all people are equal and deserve equal rights and opportunities.)

Vain: Someone who is excessively proud of their abilities, are overly preoccupied with their appearance, or thinks they are inexplicably unique.

OPPOSITE: Modest

Vainglory: An overabundance of pride in yourself or your accomplishment; excessive vanity. Typically used to describe someone who feels superior to others.

OPPOSITE: Meekness, humility, modest